S0-ARK-535

Every new generation of children is enthralled by the famous stories in our Well-Loved Tales series. Younger ones love to have the story read to them, and to examine each tiny detail of the full colour illustrations. Older children will enjoy the exciting stories in an easy-to-read text.

Revised edition

© LADYBIRD BOOKS LTD MCMLXXXII

The Musicians of Bremen

retold for easy reading
by VERA SOUTHGATE, MA BCom

illustrated by MARGARET GOLD

Ladybird Books Loughborough

In Germany there is a large town called Bremen. Not far away from Bremen is a small village. Long ago, in this village, there lived a man who had a donkey.

The donkey had worked hard for many, many years. Every day, except Sundays, he had carried heavy sacks of corn to the mill to be ground into flour. But as the donkey grew older, the sacks of

corn became too heavy for him.

Then the man began to wonder why he should go on feeding a donkey that was not strong enough to work for him.

BREMEN

The donkey knew what the man was thinking, so he decided to run away.

He liked music and he wanted to become a musician. He felt sure that a large town like Bremen would have a town band. He thought that perhaps he could earn his living by joining the musicians in the band. So he set off along the road to Bremen.

Before long, the donkey saw a dog lying by the side of the road. The dog looked tired. He lay panting as though he had run a race.

"Now then, old dog! What is the matter with you?" asked the donkey.

"Ah!" replied the dog. "I am becoming too old to hunt. My master is planning to kill me and so I have run away. But I do not know how I can earn my living."

"Why don't you join me?" asked the donkey. "I, too, have run away from my master. I shall soon be too old to carry corn and my master no longer wants to feed me. I plan to go to Bremen to become a town musician. Why don't you come along with me? I shall play the lute and you can play the drums."

The dog agreed, and the two of them set off along the road to Bremen.

Before long, the donkey and the dog saw a cat.
She was sitting by the side of the road, with a face
as long as three rainy days.

"Now then, old whiskers! What is the matter
with you?" asked the donkey.

"Ah!" replied the cat. "Now that I am getting old, my teeth are not so sharp and it is not very easy for me to catch mice. In fact, I'd much rather lie in front of the fire than catch mice. As I can no longer catch mice, my mistress is thinking of drowning me. So I have run away. But I do not know how I can earn my living."

"Why don't you join us?" asked the donkey. "We have both run away from our masters. We plan to go to Bremen to become town musicians. You must be used to singing at night. Why don't you come along with us?"

The cat agreed, and the three of them set off along the road to Bremen.

Before long, the three travellers came to a farmyard. A cock was sitting on the gate, crowing at the top of his voice.

"Now then, old cock! What is the matter with you?" asked the donkey. "Your crowing is loud enough to deafen me."

"Ah!" replied the cock. "We are to have guests for dinner on Sunday. My mistress plans to serve chicken soup, and tomorrow I am going to be killed to be made into soup. So now I am crowing as loudly as I can, while I'm still alive to do it."

"Don't worry, old cock," replied the donkey. "There is no need to die yet. Why don't you join us? We plan to go to Bremen to become town musicians. You have a good voice so you should be able to help us. Why don't you come along with us?"

The cock agreed, and the four of them continued along the road to Bremen.

As the four travellers could not reach the town of Bremen that same day, they agreed to spend the night in a forest.

The donkey and the dog lay down under a tree. The cat settled herself in the lower branches of the tree. The cock flew right to a top branch of the tree, where he thought he would be safest.

Before settling to sleep, the cock looked all around him. Far away in the distance, he thought he could see a tiny light.

"I think I can see a light in the distance," he called to his friends. "There must be a house not too far away."

"If that is so," replied the donkey, "let us go and find it, for I am not very comfortable here."

"And I wouldn't mind a few bones with some meat on them!" said the dog.

The four friends set off towards the tiny light. The nearer they got to it, the larger and brighter it became.

At last they came to a house with the light streaming out of a window. As the donkey was the tallest, he looked in at the window.

"What do you see, old donkey?" asked the cock.

"What do I see?" answered the donkey. "I see a table, set with good things to eat and drink, and some robbers sitting around it enjoying themselves."

"That sounds like the sort of thing we could do with," said the cock.

"Ah! If only we could get at that food!" said the donkey.

Then the four friends talked about how they might frighten away the robbers. At last they worked out a plan.

The donkey put his front hooves on the window-sill. The dog jumped on the donkey's back. The cat climbed onto the dog's back. And the cock perched on top of the cat.

They did all this without a sound.

Then the donkey gave the signal, by nodding his head, and they all began to make music together.

The donkey brayed, the dog barked, the cat miaowed and the cock crowed at the top of his voice. You never heard such a terrible noise in all your life!

At the same time, the four friends burst through the window, breaking all the glass. What a din that made!

The frightened robbers jumped up and rushed out into the forest.

Then the donkey, the dog, the cat and the cock, sat down at the table and ate until they could eat no more.

After this splendid meal, they put out the light and settled down to sleep.

The donkey lay down on some straw in the yard. The dog settled himself behind the door. The cat stretched out near the fire. And the cock flew up onto a beam, near the ceiling.

They were so tired after their long walk that soon they were all fast asleep.

Meanwhile the robbers were watching from some distance away. They saw the light go out in the house. By midnight all was quiet. Then they began to wonder why they had all been so frightened.

"We should not have let ourselves be frightened out of our wits," said the leader of the robbers. He then ordered one of the other robbers to go and look at the house.

The robber crept up to the house. Not a sound was to be heard. So he went quietly into the kitchen to light a candle.

In the dark he could see the bright eyes of the cat shining. He thought they were coals glowing in the fire. So he pushed his candle towards one of them to light it.

The cat did not like having something pushed towards her eye. She jumped up, hissing and spitting, and scratched the robber's face.

The robber, frightened out of his wits, rushed to the back door. There he fell over the dog, who jumped up and bit him in the leg.

As the man limped across the yard, howling, the donkey gave him a good kick.

By this time, the cock had been wakened by all
the din. He came flying down from his beam,
screeching for all he was worth.

The robber was terrified. He limped back to his friends as quickly as he could.

"Whatever happened to you?" asked the leader of the robbers.

"Oh dear!" groaned the frightened robber. "There's a witch in the house. She spat on me and scratched my face with her long claws.

"And behind the door, there stands a man with a knife. He stabbed me in the leg.

"And in the yard, there is a big, black monster. He beat me with a wooden stick.

"And up near the roof, there sits a judge. He was shouting, 'Bring the robber here to me!'

"So I ran away as quickly as I could!"

After this frightening tale, the robbers never dared to go near the house again.

This suited the four friends very well. They settled down happily to live together in the house.

And they never did get to Bremen to become the Musicians of Bremen!